T0386547

Published in 2023 by Murdoch Books, an imprint of Allen & Unwin
Vinterstjärna och iskristall
Text & Photographs © Jennie Lantz and Cecilia Möller Kirchsteiger
First published by Norstedts, Sweden, in 2022
Published by agreement with Norstedts Agency and Bennet Agency

Murdoch Books Australia
Cammeraygal Country
83 Alexander Street
Crows Nest NSW 2065
Phone: +61 (0)2 8425 0100
murdochbooks.com.au
info@murdochbooks.com.au

Murdoch Books UK
Ormond House
26–27 Boswell Street
London WC1N 3JZ
Phone: +44 (0) 20 8785 5995
murdochbooks.co.uk
info@murdochbooks.co.uk

For corporate orders and custom publishing,
contact our business development team at
salesenquiries@murdochbooks.com.au

Design: Sanna Sporrong
Photography: Cecilia Möller Kirchsteiger

Publisher: Céline Hughes
Translator: Alice E. Olsson
English-language editor: Kay Halsey
English-language designer and cover
    designer: Sarah McCoy
Production Director: Lou Playfair

ISBN 978 1 92261 680 7

A catalogue record for this
book is available from the
National Library of Australia

A catalogue record for this book is available
from the British Library

Printed by C & C Offset Printing Co. Ltd.,
China

10 9 8 7 6 5 4 3 2 1

Stars & Snowflakes

SIMPLE, SUSTAINABLE PAPERCRAFTS FOR THE FESTIVE SEASON

**JENNIE LANTZ &
CECILIA MÖLLER KIRCHSTEIGER**

murdoch books
London | Sydney

CONTENTS

FOREWORD
by Ernst Kirchsteiger

CREATIVITY IS A WONDERFUL WORD that has been of great significance in my life. It is my belief that in order for creativity to flow, we must first make time and space. For me, being creative is one of the great joys in life; it is always time well spent. We all need to do 'real' things in order to feel grounded – things that we both start and finish. Successfully bringing a project to its conclusion with a satisfying result is an exercise in time and patience. You have to give things the time they need to achieve the best results.

This stunning book shows the remarkable yet humble beauty of papercrafts. I love the simplicity of paper. It's all around us in everyday life, an inclusive material that is easy to get your hands on. So let this book inspire you to create some paper poetry!

If something doesn't work on the first try, be gentle with yourself – take a few deep breaths and try again. Then cheer yourself on and be proud when you are holding a crisp snow star in your hands.

May your creative juices flow!
Long live creativity!

Ernst Kirchsteiger

INTRODUCTION

IN YOUR HANDS, YOU ARE HOLDING THE BOOK *Stars & Snowflakes*.
Our dream was to create a beautiful book of papercrafts for everyone.
No matter your age, where you live or how much past experience you have,
you should easily be able to find the materials needed and create beautiful
works of paper. Undemanding, timeless and far from the digital world, this is
a book filled with lots of lovely papercrafts for the festive season. Some are
quick and easy, while others may require more patience. One thing they all have
in common: they should not cost a fortune to make. The biggest investment
is simply your time.

Our paths first crossed in 2014, when Cecilia was shooting an interior design
feature in Jennie's home. Over the years, there have been more and more joint
articles, published in different countries. Jennie runs the popular interior
design and craft account @vitanyanser (or 'White Shades') on Instagram,
where she frequently shares papercrafts and little glimpses into her beautiful
home. Cecilia works as a photographer, specialising in interior design stories
and lifestyle photography. Together, we have made our dream come true and
hope that these beautiful pictures, crafts and ideas will give you – our reader –
plenty of inspiration.

We wish you many wonderful, relaxing hours with this book and hope that
you will come to see crafting as something meditative and peaceful.
Free of stress.
Free of demands.
Let's do this together.

With love, Cecilia and Jennie

MATERIALS & TOOLS

One of our thoughts when making this book was that the materials should be cheap and easy to source. In fact, most of what you will need can be found in your local supermarket. You can make a lot of beautiful things out of regular baking paper, copier paper or even coffee filters. All of our crafts can be made with the simplest of paper, but you can also use finer varieties, such as crêpe paper or wallpaper.

Materials you'll need:

- Glue stick
- Stronger glue, e.g. Elmer's, PVA or all-purpose glue
- Pencil
- Ruler
- Scissors
- Clips or clothes pegs
- Thick thread or string
- Different types of paper

For each project, we indicate which type of paper we find most suitable. You are of course free to try other options, too!

BAKING PAPER
A thin paper sold in most supermarkets. Also known as parchment paper, it comes in sheets or rolls and is white or brown. Try to find a matte baking (or sandwich wrapping) paper as it's much easier to work with.

COPIER PAPER 80 GSM (20 LB)
A thin paper used for drawing or printing. Also known as copy or printer paper, it's easy to find in well-stocked supermarkets. Suitable for simpler crafts.

ART PAPER 100 GSM (26 LB)
A slightly thicker paper that provides a little more solidity and is perfect for making papercrafts. Typically found online and in well-stocked supermarkets.

HEAVYWEIGHT CARD PAPER 300 GSM (110 LB)
A thicker paper resembling light card. You'll find it online and in well-stocked craft shops.

CRÊPE PAPER 180 GSM (65 LB)

A thicker paper with structure and elasticity. This heavyweight crêpe paper is particularly suitable for making flowers or flower petals. Found online and in well-stocked craft shops.

WORKING WITH BAKING PAPER

Tips before you begin to craft your very own baking paper stars:

- It's easier to work with baking paper that comes in a roll than in sheets.
- It's easier to work with white baking paper than brown.
- Look for baking paper that is matte rather than glossy.
- When you're tracing the templates in this book, it's easier if you place a paperweight on the paper. Otherwise, it can easily slide around.
- When you begin to fold your stars, create different styles by varying the width of the folds.
- When it's time to glue the different parts together, it's best to use a glue stick. The brand doesn't matter; the key is simply to use a lot of glue. Slide the glue stick back and forth several times. Pinch the glued sides together for a few seconds or use a clip, letting go quickly. Remove any excess glue right away.

- If some of the folds don't stick, you can always re-glue them.
- On the stars, the glued side is on the back.
- Once you have glued all the parts together into a star, you can re-glue the centre with a stronger glue should you need to.
- If you would like to add a light source to your star, you'll need to use the templates twice to create a front and back.
- You can create pretty effects by combining parts from different stars.
- The time specified to make the star projects is based on 3 layers. The more layers you make, the longer it will take. If you want to make a star with lots of layers, you'll need to set aside many hours for crafting.

WHEN DARKNESS FALLS

Be inspired by the signs of autumn.

AUTUMN FLOWER

Crêpe paper has a wonderful texture that is perfect for making flower petals. Why not craft an autumn flower with crêpe paper petals and hang it on an empty wall? Choose a soft, subtle colour or perhaps one that pops.

Level of difficulty: Easy
Time needed: 3 hours
The autumn flower in the picture is made up of about 70 petals and has a diameter of 40 cm (16 in).

YOU WILL NEED:

Crêpe paper in a colour or colours of your choosing
Thicker paper
Stronger glue

INSTRUCTIONS:

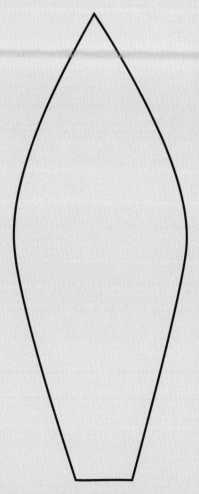

1. Cut out a template for the flower petals.
2. Trace the template onto crêpe paper, making sure that the texture of the paper aligns with the petal shape.
3. Cut out the petals just inside the lines.
4. Pull a little on the petals to make them slightly cupped.
5. Cut a circle with a diameter of your choosing from the thicker paper. Once finished, the flower should have a diameter 15 cm (6 in) bigger than the circle.
6. Start gluing the petals to the outer rim of the paper circle, with a slight overlap between each petal. Glue petals around the entire outer edge before starting the next layer, overlapping with the first.
7. Keep gluing petals in this manner until the paper circle is completely covered.
8. Your autumn flower is now ready!

LEAF STAR

When the light fades and the days grow shorter, a leaf star is a lovely decoration to light up your home. If you don't have the time or patience to make a whole star, you can craft beautiful autumn leaves from all four templates by following steps 1–6.

Level of difficulty: Medium

Time needed: 5 hours

Either make individual leaves (steps 1–6)

or combine several parts to make

a leaf star with a 38 cm (15 in) diameter.

To make a leaf star you'll need:

1 star from template 2: 7 or 8 cut-outs

1 star from template 3: 7 or 8 cut-outs

2 stars from template 4: 2 x 7 or 8 cut-outs

The glued folds will be on the back of the star and cut-outs.

YOU WILL NEED:

Brown baking paper

Thicker paper

Glue stick

Stronger glue

INSTRUCTIONS:

1. Trace the templates you want to use onto baking paper. You'll need to make them doubled. The most efficient way is to use a sheet of baking paper folded in half, aligning the long, straight side of the template with the fold.
2. Cut out the leaves just inside the lines and unfold.
3. Now fold the paper leaves like an accordion, with each fold about 1 cm (½ in) wide. Start from the longest straight side.
4. Glue the long outside of the accordion with a glue stick.
5. Now fold the accordion in half, so that the glued surface is folded in on itself. Hold for a moment, until the sides stick together.

6. Unfold and make sure that only the long sides in the middle are sticking.
7. Follow steps 1–6 for all the leaves, then assemble each star individually by following steps 8–10.
8. Assemble the leaves in pairs by gluing the short outer sides. Hold for a moment, until the sides stick together. Then unfold to check that only the short outer sides are sticking.
9. Continue assembling the leaves into groups of 3 or 4 by gluing the short outer sides as in step 8.
10. Glue all 7 or 8 leaves together to form a complete star.
11. Cut out a circle for each star, except the smallest star made from template 2. This will help support the stars and make it easier to assemble the layers. Apply a stronger glue to the centre of each star and glue on a paper circle.
12. Now glue the stars together using a stronger glue, applying it to the paper circle on each star. Then assemble the whole star and let the glue harden.
13. If you would like a light source in your leaf star, make 2 stars and follow the instructions under 'Lighting for Stars' on page 83.

TEMPLATE: LEAF STAR

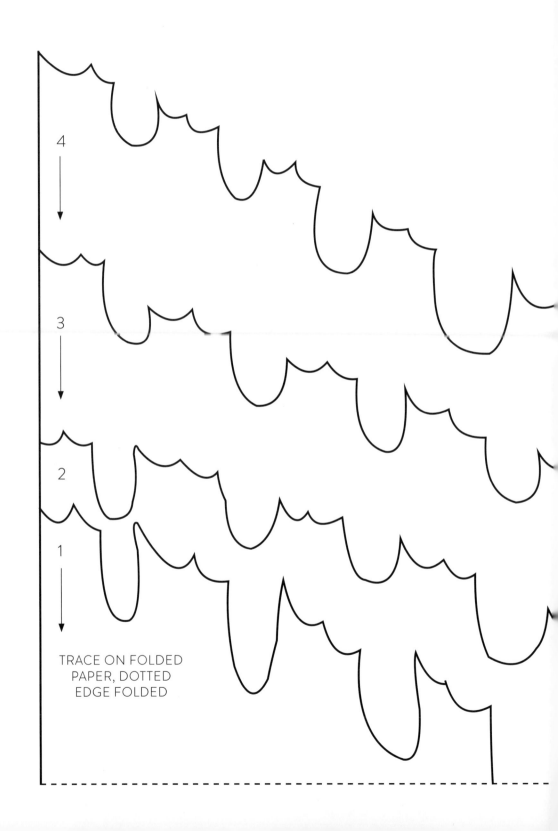

4

3

2

1

TRACE ON FOLDED
PAPER, DOTTED
EDGE FOLDED

COPY THE TEMPLATES ON A SCALE OF 1:1 (100%).
OF COURSE, THE SCALE CAN ALSO BE
ADJUSTED TO CHANGE THE SIZE.

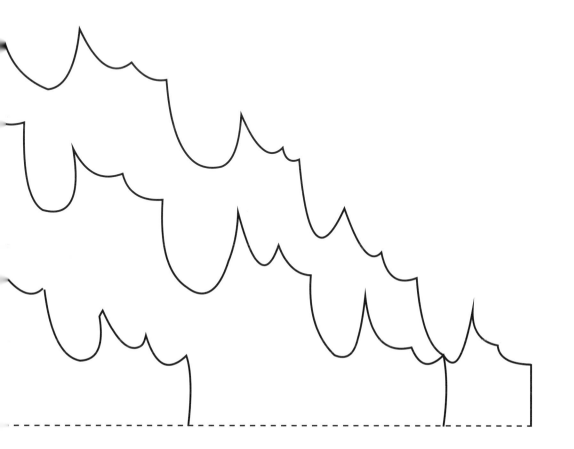

AUTUMN WREATH

Craft a wreath that is as simple as it is beautiful. It's up to you how bushy you want your wreath to be. Changing the style is easy because the leaves are just attached with pins. When it's time to put it away until next year, remove the pins and store the leaves and the straw base separately.

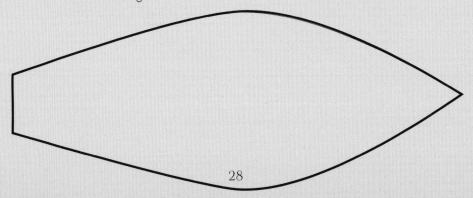

Level of difficulty: Easy
Time needed: 4 hours
The wreath pictured is made up of about 70 leaves pinned onto a base 37 cm (14½ in) in diameter.

YOU WILL NEED:
Crêpe paper in a colour or colours of your choosing
A wreath base made of straw
Sewing pins
Ribbon for hanging

INSTRUCTIONS:
1. Cut out a template for the leaves.
2. Trace the template onto crêpe paper, making sure that the texture of the paper aligns with the leaf shape.
3. Cut out the leaves just inside the lines.
4. Pull a little on the leaves to make them slightly cupped.
5. Pin the leaves onto the wreath with a slight overlap. Continue all the way round.
6. Tie a ribbon around the wreath — now it's ready to hang!
7. The leaves may need to be adjusted so that they are at an even angle around the wreath once it's hung.

FALLEN LEAVES

Gather beautiful autumn leaves from the garden or create your own from paper that will last year after year. Why not make a whole pile of fallen leaves to string into a garland or sprinkle over the dinner table?

Level of difficulty: Easy
Time needed: 15 minutes

YOU WILL NEED:
Paper in a colour or colours
of your choosing
Glue stick

INSTRUCTIONS:
1. Cut a more or less equilateral triangle with the sides all the same length out of paper. Choose the size you want – the height of the leaf will be half the length of the triangle.
2. Fold half the triangle like an accordion. If you are using crêpe paper, make sure that the texture of the paper is aligned with the folds.
3. Cut off the unfolded top of the triangle.
4. Glue the long side of the accordion that you folded first.
5. Now fold the accordion in half, so that the glued surface is folded in on itself. Pinch and hold for a moment, until you can feel that the glue is sticking on the entire surface.
6. Unfold a beautiful autumn leaf!

ADVENT
SEASON

Let stars of all shapes create an atmospheric December.

ICE CRYSTAL

The ice crystal is an evenly circular advent star with soft, rounded tips. It has the easiest template of all the advent stars and is perfect to start with if this is your first time making a star out of baking paper.

Level of difficulty: Medium

Time needed: 4 hours (for a star with 3 layers)

The finished ice crystal is thick, so it's best made with a maximum of 3 layers.

For instance, choose templates 1, 2 and 3 for a small ice crystal (14 cm/5½ in diameter) and templates 4, 5 and 6 for a large ice crystal (41 cm/16 in diameter).

An ice crystal with only 2 layers is beautiful, too — for example, templates 1 and 4.

Or why not make lots of ice crystals from template 1 and hang them in a garland?

Ice crystal from template 1 (4 cm/1½ in diameter): 4 cut-outs folded vertically

Ice crystal from template 2 (9 cm/3½ in diameter): 4 cut-outs folded vertically

Ice crystal from template 3 (14 cm/5½ in diameter): 4 cut-outs folded vertically

Ice crystal from template 4 (20 cm/8 in diameter): 4 cut-outs folded vertically

Ice crystal from template 5 (30 cm/12 in diameter): 4 cut-outs folded horizontally

Ice crystal from template 6 (41 cm/16 in diameter): 4 cut-outs folded horizontally

The glued folds will be on the back of the star and cut-outs.

YOU WILL NEED:

White baking paper

Thicker paper

Glue stick

Stronger glue

INSTRUCTIONS:

1. Trace the templates you want to use onto baking paper. You'll need to make them doubled as instructed on the template.

2. Cut out the pieces from the baking paper just inside the lines.

3. Fold the paper pieces like an accordion, with each fold about 2.5 cm (1 inch) wide. Templates 1–4 are folded vertically, while templates 5 and 6 are folded horizontally.

4. Fold the accordions in half and round the corners by cutting about 1.5 cm (⅝ in) down from the top. You can vary the style of your ice crystal by not shaping the corners at all or by making them pointy — but make sure to be consistent across all the pieces.

5. Now complete steps 6–8 for each piece, one at a time.

6. Thoroughly coat the entire inside of the folded accordion with a glue stick.

7. Pinch the folded accordion together, so that the glued surface is folded in on itself. Hold for a moment, until the sides stick together.

8. Unfold and make sure that only the glued sides are sticking.

9. Now assemble each ice crystal individually by first gluing the accordions together in pairs. Hold for a moment, until the sides stick together. Then unfold and make sure that only the glued sides are sticking.

10. Glue 2 pairs of accordions together to form a whole ice crystal.

11. Cut out 2 circles for each ice crystal in a thicker paper to help stabilise the crystal and make it easier to assemble the layers. Glue a paper circle to the centre on both the front and back of each ice crystal with a stronger glue. The smallest ice crystal will sit as the top layer and should only have a paper circle on the back.

12. Now assemble the layers of the ice crystal using a stronger glue that you apply to the paper circle on each crystal. Then place the ice crystals on top of each other and let the glue harden.

13. If you would like a light source in your ice crystal, make 2 identical crystals and follow the instructions under 'Lighting for Stars' on page 83.

TEMPLATE: ICE CRYSTAL

Template 6 (A4 size)
Trace on folded paper,
dotted edge folded

↓

Then fold horizontally

Template 5 Trace on folded paper, dotted edge folded ← Then fold horizontally

Template 4
Trace on folded paper,
dotted edge folded

↓

Then fold vertically

COPY THE TEMPLATES ON A SCALE OF 1:1 (100%).
OF COURSE, THE SCALE CAN ALSO BE
ADJUSTED TO CHANGE THE SIZE.

Template 3
Trace on folded paper,
dotted edge folded

↓

Then fold vertically

Template 2
Trace on folded paper,
dotted edge folded

↓

Then fold vertically

Template 1
Trace on folded paper,
dotted edge folded

↓

Then fold vertically

SNOWFLAKE

The symmetry of a snowflake is celebrated in this advent star. With its rounded pattern, it creates a soft and inviting impression.

Level of difficulty: Medium

Time needed: 4 hours (for a star with 3 layers)

The finished snowflake is thick, so it's best made in 3 layers — though it looks great with more layers, too. For instance, choose templates 1, 3 and 5 or templates 2, 4 and 6 if you want to make it in 3 layers.

Snowflake from template 1 (21 cm/8¼ in diameter): 3 cut-outs

Snowflake from template 2 (29 cm/11½ in diameter): 3 cut-outs

Snowflake from template 3 (36 cm/14¼ in diameter): 3 cut-outs

Snowflake from template 4 (42 cm/16½ in diameter): 4 cut-outs

Snowflake from template 5 (50 cm/20 in diameter): 5 cut-outs

Snowflake from template 6 (58 cm/23 in diameter): 5 cut-outs

The glued folds will be on the back of the star and cut-outs.

YOU WILL NEED:

White baking paper

Thicker paper

Glue stick

Stronger glue

INSTRUCTIONS:

1. Trace the templates you want to use onto baking paper. You'll need to make them doubled as instructed on the template.

2. Cut out the pieces from the baking paper just inside the lines.

3. Fold the paper pieces like an accordion, with each fold about 2.5 cm (1 inch) wide.

4. Fold the accordions in half. Then complete steps 5–7 for each piece, one at a time.

5. Thoroughly coat the entire inside of the folded accordion with a glue stick.

6. Now pinch the folded accordion together, so that the glued surface is folded in on itself. Hold for a moment, until the sides stick together.

7. Unfold and make sure that only the glued sides are sticking.

8. Now assemble each snowflake individually by first gluing 2 accordions together. Hold for a moment, until the sides stick together. Then unfold and make sure that only the glued sides are sticking.

9. Glue the accordions together, depending on the templates chosen, to form a whole snowflake.

10. Cut out 2 circles for each snowflake in a thicker paper to help stabilise the snowflake and make it easier to assemble the layers. Glue a paper circle to the centre on both the front and back of each snowflake with a stronger glue. The smallest snowflake will sit as the top layer and should only have a paper circle on the back.

11. Now assemble the layers of the snowflake using a stronger glue that you apply to the paper circle on each snowflake. Then place the snowflakes on top of each other and let the glue harden.

12. If you would like a light source in your snowflake, make 2 identical snowflakes and then follow the instructions under 'Lighting for Stars' on page 83.

TEMPLATE: SNOWFLAKE

6   5   4   3

2

1

COPY THE TEMPLATES
ON A SCALE OF 1:1 (100%).
OF COURSE, THE SCALE
CAN ALSO BE ADJUSTED
TO CHANGE THE SIZE.

TRACE ON FOLDED PAPER,
DOTTED EDGE FOLDED

HOAR FROST

Hoar frost is an advent star with tips of different lengths. Because the tips have a wider and rounder shape, it creates a wispy outline while still looking sharp.

Level of difficulty: Medium
Time needed: 3 hours (for a star with 3 layers)
Hoar frost is beautiful in 3 layers but also works well using only templates 1 and 3.
Hoar frost from template 1
(36 cm/14¼ in diameter): 4 cut-outs
Hoar frost from template 2
(48 cm/19 in diameter): 4 cut-outs
Hoar frost from template 3
(59 cm/23¼ in diameter): 5 cut-outs
The glued folds will be on the back of the star and cut-outs.

YOU WILL NEED:
White baking paper
Thicker paper
Glue stick
Stronger glue

INSTRUCTIONS:
1. Trace the templates you want to use onto baking paper. You'll need to make them doubled as instructed on the template.
2. Cut out the pieces from the baking paper just inside the lines.
3. Fold the paper pieces like an accordion, where each fold is about 2.5 cm (1 inch) wide.
4. Fold the accordions in half, then complete steps 5–7 for each piece, one at a time.
5. Thoroughly coat the entire inside of the folded accordion with a glue stick.

6. Now pinch the folded accordion together, so that the glued surface is folded in on itself. Hold for a moment, until the sides stick together.

7. Unfold and make sure that only the glued sides are sticking.

8. Now assemble each hoar frost star individually by first gluing 2 accordions together. Hold for a moment, until the sides stick together. Then unfold and make sure that only the glued sides are sticking.

9. Glue the accordions together, depending on the templates chosen, to form a whole hoar frost star.

10. Cut out 2 circles for each hoar frost star in a thicker paper to help stabilise the star and make it easier to assemble the layers. Glue a paper circle to the centre on both the front and back of each star with a stronger glue. The smallest star will sit as the top layer and should only have a paper circle on the back.

11. Now assemble the layers of the hoar frost star using a stronger glue that you apply to the paper circle on each star. Then place the stars on top of each other and let the glue harden.

12. If you would like a light source in your hoar frost star, make 2 identical stars and follow the instructions under 'Lighting for Stars' on page 83.

TEMPLATE: HOAR FROST

3

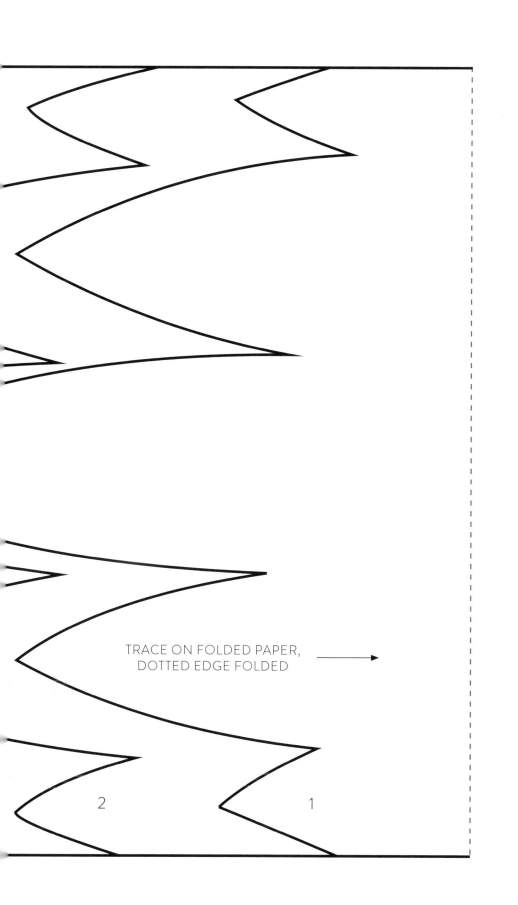

TRACE ON FOLDED PAPER,
DOTTED EDGE FOLDED

2

1

SNOW STAR

The snow star is the advent star with the most templates in different sizes. Since the number of layers and pieces you choose to make changes the appearance of the star, play around with it until you find the combination you like best.

Level of difficulty: Medium
Time needed: 4 hours (for a star with 3 layers)
Star from template 1 (12 cm/4½ in diameter): 5 cut-outs
Star from template 2 (16 cm/6¼ in diameter): 5 cut-outs
Star from template 3 (20 cm/8 in diameter): 5 cut-outs
Star from template 4 (24 cm/9½ in diameter): 5 cut-outs
Star from template 5 (28 cm/11 in diameter): 5 cut-outs
Star from template 6 (32 cm/12½ in diameter): 5 cut-outs
Star from template 7 (36 cm/14¼ in diameter): 5 cut-outs
Star from template 8 (40 cm/16 in diameter): 10 cut-outs
Star from template 9 (49 cm/19¼ in diameter): 10 cut-outs
Star from template 10 (59 cm/23¼ in diameter): 10 cut-outs
The glued folds will be on the back of the star and cut-outs.

YOU WILL NEED:
White baking paper
Thicker paper
Glue stick
Stronger glue

INSTRUCTIONS:
1. Trace the templates you want to use onto baking paper.
   You'll need to make them doubled as instructed on the template.
2. Cut out the pieces from the baking paper just inside the lines.
3. Fold the paper pieces horizontally like an accordion, with each fold about 1–1.5 cm (½–⅝ in) wide.
4. Fold the accordions in half, then complete steps 5–7 for each piece, one at a time.

5. Thoroughly coat the entire inside of the folded accordion with a glue stick.

6. Now pinch the folded accordion together, so that the glued surface is folded in on itself. Hold for a moment, until the sides stick together.

7. Unfold and make sure that only the glued sides are sticking.

8. Now assemble each snow star individually by first gluing the accordions together in pairs. Hold for a moment, until the sides stick together. Then unfold and make sure that only the glued sides are sticking.

9. Glue the accordions together to form a snow star by first gluing them in double pairs, depending on the templates chosen, then into a complete snow star.

10. Cut out 2 circles for each snow star in a thicker paper to help stabilise the star and make it easier to assemble the layers.

11. Glue a paper circle to the centre on both the front and back of each star with a stronger glue. The smallest star will sit as the top layer and should only have a paper circle on the back.

12. Now assemble the layers of the snow star using a stronger glue that you apply to the paper circle on each star. Then place the snow stars on top of each other and let the glue harden.

13. If you would like a light source in your snow star, make 2 identical stars and follow the instructions under 'Lighting for Stars' on page 83.

TEMPLATE: SNOW STAR

TRACE ON
FOLDED PAPER,
DOTTED EDGE
FOLDED →

TEMPLATE: SNOW STAR

COPY THE TEMPLATES ON A SCALE OF 1:1 (100%).
OF COURSE, THE SCALE CAN ALSO BE
ADJUSTED TO CHANGE THE SIZE.

10

TRACE ON FOLDED PAPER,
DOTTED EDGE FOLDED ⟶

9

8

POLE STAR

The pole star has symmetrically shaped tips and is made up of many cut-outs. Let it light up your window to create a lovely festive atmosphere for those who pass by your home, too.

Level of difficulty: Medium/advanced

Time needed: 6 hours (for a star with 3 layers)

The pole star consists of many pieces that need to be glued together to create its signature appearance. You can use fewer pieces for each pole star — for instance: 6 cut-outs from templates 1, 2 and 3, and 8 cut-outs from templates 4 and 5. This is quicker but also gives the pole star a different look.

Star from template 1 (15 cm/6 in diameter): 8 cut-outs

Star from template 2 (22 cm/8½ in diameter): 10 cut-outs

Star from template 3 (30 cm/12 in diameter): 12 cut-outs

Star from template 4 (37 cm/14½ in diameter): 14 cut-outs

Star from template 5 (44 cm/17½ in diameter): 16 cut-outs

Star from template 6 (52 cm/20½ in diameter): 18 cut-outs

Star from template 7 (59 cm/23¼ in diameter): 20 cut-outs

The glued folds will be on the back of the star and cut-outs.

YOU WILL NEED:

White baking paper

Thicker paper

Glue stick

Stronger glue

INSTRUCTIONS:

1. Trace the templates you want to use onto baking paper. You'll need to make them doubled as instructed on the template.
2. Cut out the pieces from baking paper just inside the lines, making sure that the tips are pointy.
3. Fold the paper pieces horizontally like an accordion, with each fold about 1–1.5 cm (½–⅝ in) wide.

4. Fold all the accordions in half. Then complete steps 5–7 for each piece, one at a time.

5. Thoroughly coat the entire inside of the folded accordion with a glue stick.

6. Now pinch the folded accordion together, so that the glued surface is folded in on itself. Hold for a moment, until the sides stick together.

7. Unfold and make sure that only the glued sides are sticking.

8. Now assemble each pole star individually by first gluing the accordions together in pairs, then double pairs, before finally assembling the whole star. Hold for a moment, until the sides stick together. Then unfold and make sure that only the glued sides are sticking.

9. Cut out 2 circles for each pole star in a thicker paper to help stabilise the star and make it easier to assemble the layers.

10. Glue a paper circle to the centre on both the front and back of each star with a stronger glue. The smallest star will sit as the top layer and should only have a paper circle on the back.

11. Now assemble the layers of the pole star using a stronger glue that you apply to the paper circle on each star. Then place the pole stars on top of each other and let the glue harden.

12. If you would like a light source in your pole star, make 2 identical stars and follow the instructions under 'Lighting for Stars' on page 83.

TEMPLATE: POLE STAR

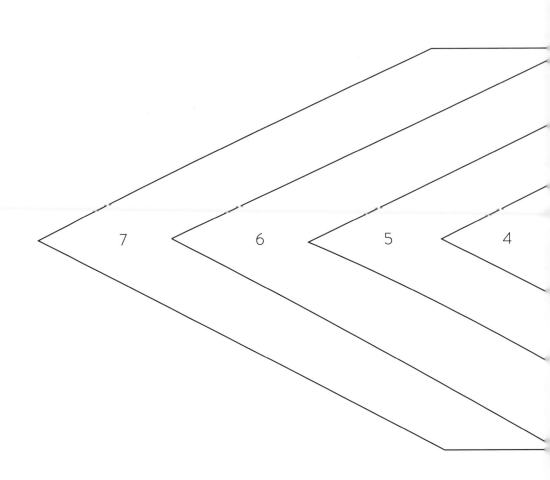

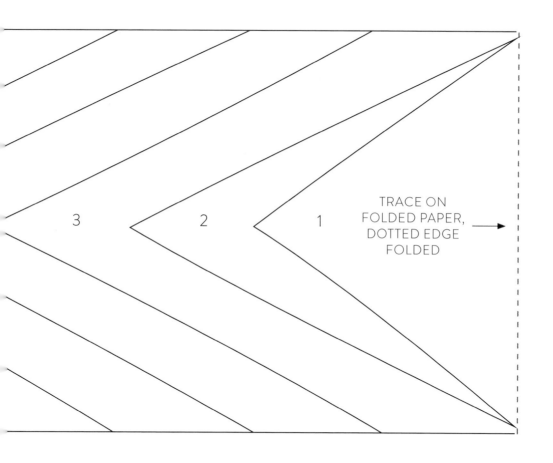

COPY THE TEMPLATES ON A SCALE OF 1:1 (100%). OF COURSE, THE SCALE CAN ALSO BE ADJUSTED TO CHANGE THE SIZE.

3

2

1

TRACE ON
FOLDED PAPER,
DOTTED EDGE
FOLDED →

ICICLE

Icicles are created when dripping water freezes. This phenomenon has inspired us to create the icicle advent star, with its sprawling, pointy, irregular tips.

Level of difficulty: Medium
Time needed: 4 hours (for a star with 3 layers)
The icicle star has a slightly more sprawling look because of its pointy, irregular tips. For this reason, the pieces take a little longer to cut. The icicle star can be made using all 5 templates, but also works well using only 2 or 3.
Icicle from template 1 (29 cm/11½ in diameter): 7 cut-outs
Icicle from template 2 (37 cm/14½ in diameter): 7 cut-outs
Icicle from template 3 (44 cm/17½ in diameter): 7 cut-outs
Icicle from template 4 (52 cm/20½ in diameter): 7 cut-outs
Icicle from template 5 (59 cm/23¼ in diameter): 7 cut-outs
The glued folds will be on the back of the star
and cut-outs.

YOU WILL NEED:
White baking paper
Thicker paper
Glue stick
Stronger glue

INSTRUCTIONS:
1. Trace the templates you want to use onto baking paper. You'll need to make them doubled as instructed on the template.
2. Cut out the pieces from baking paper just inside the lines, making sure that the tips are pointy.
3. Starting from the longest side, fold the paper pieces horizontally, like an accordion, with each fold about 1–1.5 cm (½–⅝ in) wide.
4. Fold the accordions in half with the shortest side facing inward. Then complete steps 5–7 for each piece, one at a time.

5. Thoroughly coat the entire inside of the folded accordion with a glue stick.

6. Now pinch the folded accordion together, so that the glued surface is folded in on itself. Hold for a moment, until the sides stick together.

7. Unfold and make sure that only the glued sides are sticking.

8. Now assemble each icicle individually by first gluing the accordions together in pairs. Hold for a moment, until the sides stick together. Then unfold and make sure that only the glued sides are sticking.

9. Glue the accordions together to form an icicle star by first gluing them in double pairs, then into a complete star.

10. Cut out 2 circles for each icicle in a thicker paper to help stabilise the star and make it easier to assemble the layers.

11. Glue a paper circle to the centre on both the front and back of each icicle with a stronger glue. The smallest icicle will sit as the top layer and should only have a paper circle on the back.

12. Now assemble the layers of the icicle using a stronger glue that you apply to the paper circle on each icicle. Then place the icicles on top of each other and let the glue harden.

13. If you would like a light source in your icicle star, make 2 identical stars and follow the instructions under 'Lighting for Stars' on page 83.

TEMPLATE: ICICLE

COPY THE TEMPLATES ON A SCALE OF 1:1 (100%).
OF COURSE, THE SCALE CAN ALSO BE
ADJUSTED TO CHANGE THE SIZE.

5

4

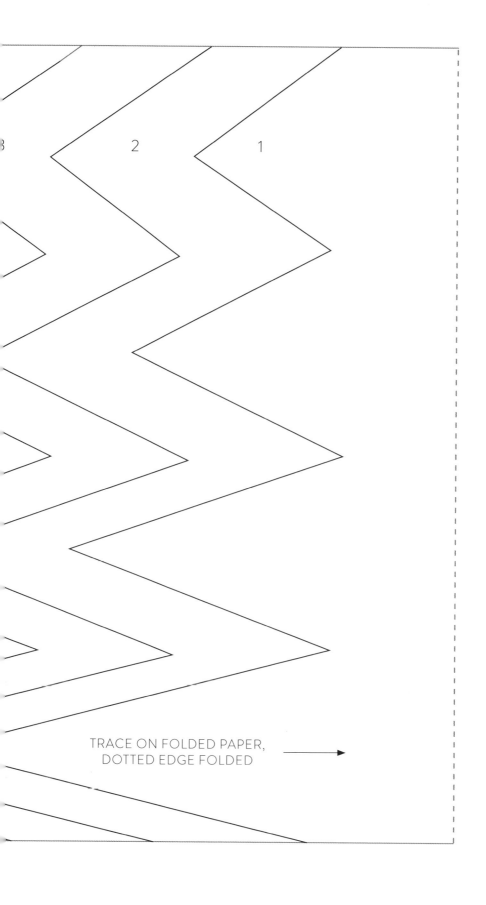

3

2

1

TRACE ON FOLDED PAPER,
DOTTED EDGE FOLDED

BAG STAR

Decorate your home with bag stars, which are both quick and easy to make. They look just as nice whether they are hanging or standing in a window — or why not place them on a shelf?

Level of difficulty: Easy
Time needed: 30 minutes

YOU WILL NEED:
8 flat-bottomed paper bags (12 x 20 cm/4½ x 8 in)
Glue stick
Ribbon for hanging

INSTRUCTIONS:

1. Create your template exactly the way you want it. Make the template pointy or round, with or without holes on the sides – see the examples opposite.
2. Trace the template onto 8 folded paper bags and cut them out, leaving the bottom of the bags intact.
3. Glue a line down the middle of each bag and horizontally along the bottom. The glued lines should form an upside-down T.
4. In this way, glue 7 bags together, placing them on top of each other in a pile.
5. If you want a ribbon for hanging your bag star, glue it between bags 7 and 8.
6. When all 8 bags have been glued together, pull the star into shape and glue the last 2 sides.

It's not possible to put a light source in a bag star.

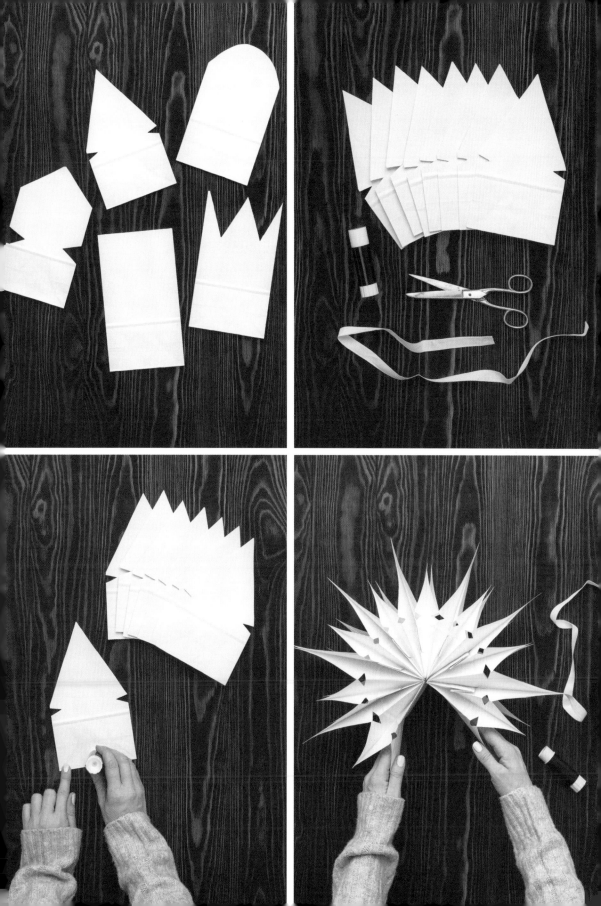

LIGHTING FOR STARS

Handcrafting advent stars from baking paper takes time and requires patience. They deserve to be displayed in your window in all their luminous brilliance.

Level of difficulty: Medium

Time needed: 1 hour

In order to mount a light source in an advent star made of baking paper, you'll need 2 identical stars made from the same templates. The biggest pieces, sitting right up against the light source, need to be at least 30 cm (12 in) in diameter. We recommend that you make your stars or crystals with at least 3 layers. The pictures on the left show a 5-layer snow star (see page 59).

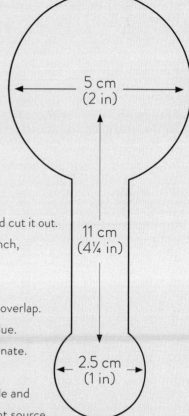

YOU WILL NEED:
Heavyweight card paper

Thicker paper

Stronger glue

Cord with light socket

Small LED light bulb, about 2.3 W

INSTRUCTIONS:
1. Cut out a 7 x 50 cm (2¾ x 20 in) strip of card paper.
2. Trace the light source template onto the centre of the strip and cut it out.
3. Make holes along the sides of the paper strip using a hole punch, except where the paper has been cut out.
4. Cut out 2 x 20 cm (8 in) circles from the thicker paper.
5. Bend the paper strip into a circle and staple it in place at the overlap.
6. Glue a paper circle to each side of the strip with a stronger glue.
7. On each paper circle, glue one of the stars you want to illuminate. Let the glue harden.
8. Mount the light source by threading it through the bigger hole and sliding it to the smaller one. Use a small LED bulb as your light source. **Make sure that the bulb is not touching the paper.** In the picture, only one paper circle and star have been glued together to show how the bulb should be positioned.
9. Your star is now ready to be hung!

CHRISTMAS SPIRIT

Decorate your tree with garlands and ornaments.

CHRISTMAS TREE TOPPER

There are those who think that a Christmas tree is not complete without a star on top. Everyone should follow their own taste — but should you want a Christmas tree topper in the shape of a star, you can make it out of paper.

Level of difficulty: Medium
Time needed: 1 hour

YOU WILL NEED:

Thicker paper
Glue stick
Stronger glue

INSTRUCTIONS:

1. Cut out 2 x 20 cm (8 in) square sheets of paper and complete steps 2–6 for each sheet.
2. Fold the sheet into a triangle, corner to corner. Unfold and fold it once more to make another triangle, this time along the other diagonal. Unfold.
3. Fold the sheet in half, unfold, then fold it in half the other way, then unfold once more. You have now created 8 folds radiating out from the centre of the sheet.
4. Cut about 5 cm (2 in) into the sheet along the 4 folds that run perpendicular to the edge of the paper.
5. Create triangles in each corner of the sheet by folding from the cuts towards the nearest fold.
6. Glue one side of the triangle and place the other side over it to create the tips of the star. Repeat until the sheet has 4 tips.
7. You now have 2 x 4-pointed stars.
8. Make a cone out of A4-sized thicker paper by folding one of the corners and rolling it into a cone (see picture on the next page).
9. Glue the edge of the cone to secure its shape.

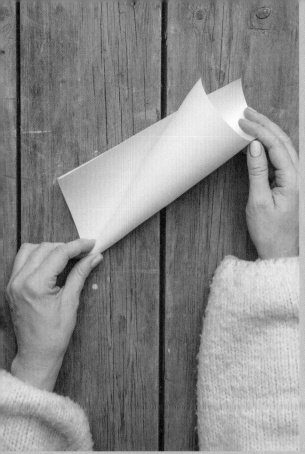

10. Give the cone a flat base.
11. Glue the cone with the tip facing upward to the inside of one of the stars with a stronger glue.
12. Finally, glue the inside of the other star to the cone, making it overlap with the first star.

BOOK TREE

Finally, a papercraft you can make out of all those cheap books at the flea market. Paperback or hardcover, it doesn't matter — just choose a book according to the size you want for your tree.

Level of difficulty: Easy
Time needed: 30 minutes

YOU WILL NEED:

A book
Optional: star, glue stick, toothpick

INSTRUCTIONS:

1. Remove the covers from the book, leaving only the pages.
2. Divide the book into sections of 40–70 pages each. The number of pages will determine how dense the tree is.
3. Fold the top right corner of the first page down towards the spine of the book.
4. Then fold the diagonal edge now created down towards the spine of the book.
5. Fold up the flap sticking out below the book.
6. Unfold the page to hide the flap.
7. Refold the page the way it was folded in step 4.
8. Turn the page and repeat steps 3–7 for the remaining pages. When all the pages are folded, shape the book into a standing Christmas tree.
9. If you want a star on top of your book tree, cut out 2 paper stars and glue them together with a toothpick in between.
10. Stick the star into the top of the book tree.

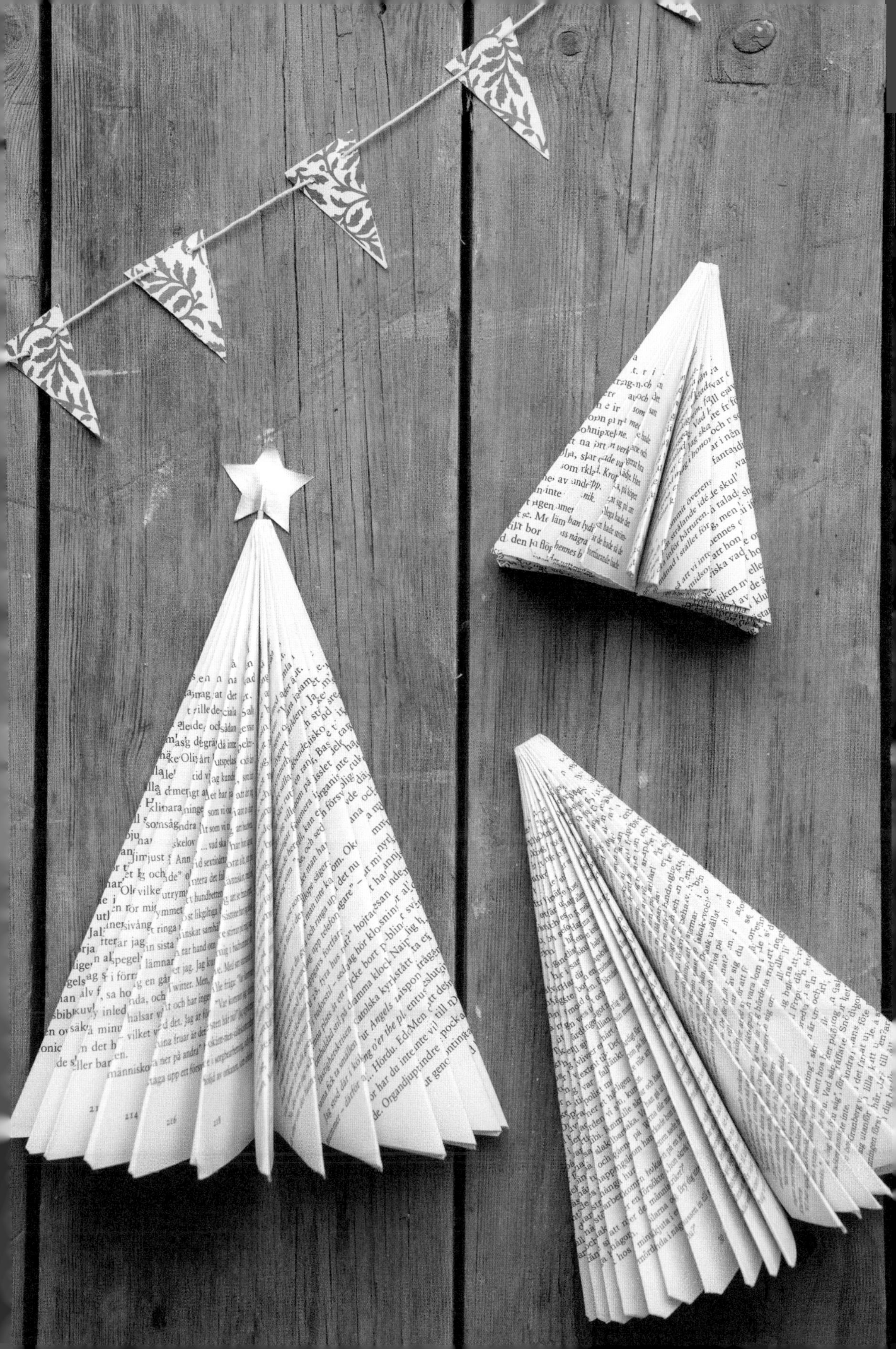

GARLANDS

Make your Christmas more festive with garlands in all shapes and colours!
These are perfect for decorating your tree, or why not hang them on the
wall or above the dining table? If you need ideas for how to shape your
garland, cookie cutters make perfect templates.

Level of difficulty: Easy
Time needed: 1 hour

YOU WILL NEED:

Thicker paper in a colour and/or pattern of your choosing
Needle and thick thread or string
Glue stick

INSTRUCTIONS:

1. Cut out a template in the desired shape and
   size for your garland.
2. If you have chosen a paper that only has a
   pattern on one side, you'll need to glue the
   backs of 2 sheets together.
3. Trace the template onto your chosen paper
   and cut out lots of it.
4. Make 2 small holes in each piece and string
   them together on a thread.
5. Choose the distance you want between each
   piece, then hang your garland.
6. If you want to make a paper chain, start by
   cutting lots of strips of paper. Take one strip
   and glue it into a loop. Next, glue another
   strip into a loop, passing it through the first.
   Repeat until your chain is the desired length.

PAPER ANGELS

Make your own beautiful angels to hang from the tree out of paper in a colour and pattern of your choosing. A papercraft so simple, anyone can do it.

Level of difficulty: Easy
Time needed: 30 minutes

There are 2 ways to make a paper angel: either with a round fold to create the angel's head or with a tiny ball. Use paper that is a little thicker than regular wrapping paper.

YOU WILL NEED:

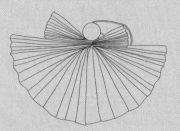

Thicker paper in a colour and/or pattern of your choosing
Thick thread or string
Glue stick
A pencil or a compressed paper ball for the angel's head

INSTRUCTIONS:

1. Cut out 2 sheets of paper in a colour and/or pattern of your choosing. One sheet needs to be wider than the other, while both should be the same length. For example, the large sheet can be A4 size and the smaller sheet the length of an A4 sheet but only 15 cm (6 in) wide.
2. Fold the large sheet in half lengthways, then twice more in the same direction.
3. Unfold and use the folds in the sheet as a guide to make straight folds for your angel (see picture on the next page).
4. Now fold the sheet like an accordion. Repeat steps 2–4 for the smaller sheet.
5. If you want to cut a pattern on the angel's body, now is the time. For instance, you can make the ends of the accordion pointy or curved or cut little holes along the sides.
6. Follow steps 7–9 to make an angel without a ball for a head or steps 10–14 if using a ball.

7. Place the 2 accordions on top of each other with a pencil in the middle underneath. Fold the accordions over the pencil so that they wrap around it.

8. Wrap a piece of string a few times around the accordions below the pencil and tie a knot to create the angel's head.

9. Remove the pencil, then unfold the angel's arms and dress. Glue the angel's dress together.

10. Fold the larger accordion in half.

11. Thread the ball that will become the angel's head onto a piece of string and place the ball in the middle on top of the smaller accordion, which in turn sits on top of the larger accordion.

12. Wrap the string around the middle of the accordions, back up the other side and through the ball once more.

13. Tighten the string to create the angel's arms and dress. Tie the ball in place.

14. Glue the angel's dress together.

WINTER STAR

A simple winter star that is quick and easy to make. Try folding it out of wrapping paper, wallpaper or thicker art paper. The star can easily be made in different variations by changing the size, number of folds or pattern.

Level of difficulty: Easy
Time needed: 30 minutes

YOU WILL NEED:

Paper in a colour and/or pattern of your choosing
Thick thread or string
Glue stick

INSTRUCTIONS:

1. Cut out a sheet at least twice as long as it is wide. If you want to make a star with denser folds, make the sheet even longer. The width of the paper will be the same as the diameter and size of the star.
2. Fold the sheet in half lengthways, then twice more in the same direction.
3. Unfold and use the folds in the sheet as a guide to make straight folds for your star.
4. Now fold the sheet like an accordion.
5. Fold the accordion in half, then unfold it again.

6. Tie a thread or string around the middle of the accordion.
7. Choose whether you want to cut patterns in your star or shape the tips. You can choose to cut pointy or rounded tips.
8. Glue the long sides of the accordion.
9. Unfold the star so that the glued sides meet and stick to each other. If you want to hang your star, this is the time to attach a piece of string.

CHRISTMAS BAUBLES

A new take on Christmas baubles — here made of paper. Why not start a new tradition and make a fresh template every year? Or perhaps try a different colour or pattern?

Level of difficulty: Easy
Time needed: 1 hour
The finished Christmas baubles are about 8 cm (3¼ in) in diameter and 10 cm (4 in) high.

YOU WILL NEED:

Thicker paper
Glue stick
Stronger glue
String or ribbon for hanging

INSTRUCTIONS:

1. Choose which type of bauble you want to make.
2. Fold the paper in half, then trace the template onto the paper, lining up the long side of the template with the folded edge of the paper before tracing and cutting. You'll need 25 pieces for each ornament.
3. Glue a thin line along the folded edge of each piece and place them on top of each other, making them stick together.
4. Once you have glued all the pieces together, glue string to the side with all the folded edges.
5. Assemble the bauble by applying a stronger glue along the side with all the folded edges, then unfolding the bauble so that the sides meet and stick to each other.

TEMPLATE: CHRISTMAS BAUBLES

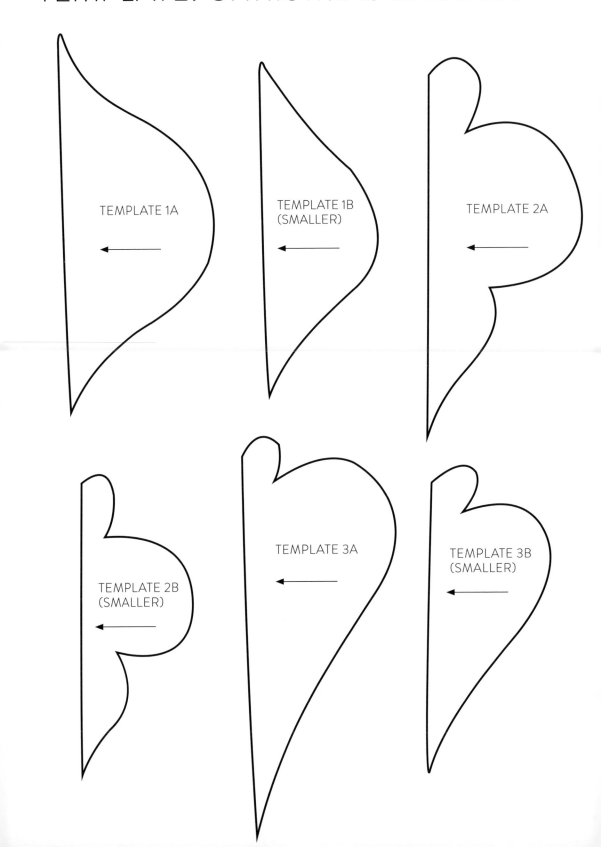

TEMPLATE 1A

TEMPLATE 1B
(SMALLER)

TEMPLATE 2A

TEMPLATE 2B
(SMALLER)

TEMPLATE 3A

TEMPLATE 3B
(SMALLER)

TEMPLATE 4A

←

TEMPLATE 4B
(SMALLER)

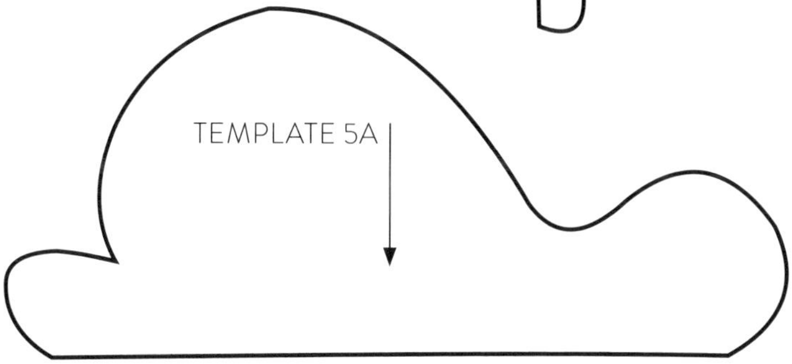

←

TEMPLATE 5A

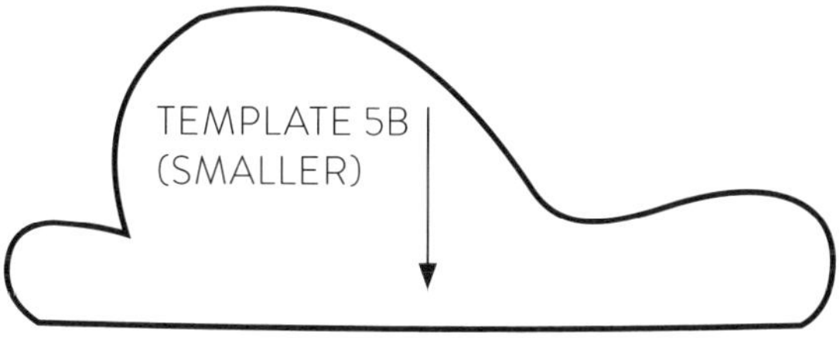

↓

TEMPLATE 5B
(SMALLER)

↓

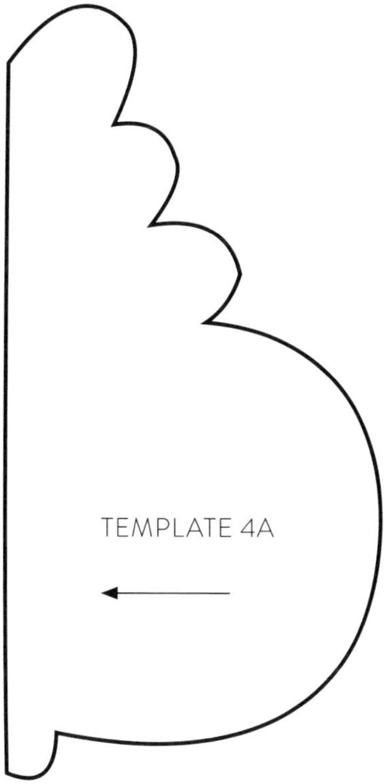

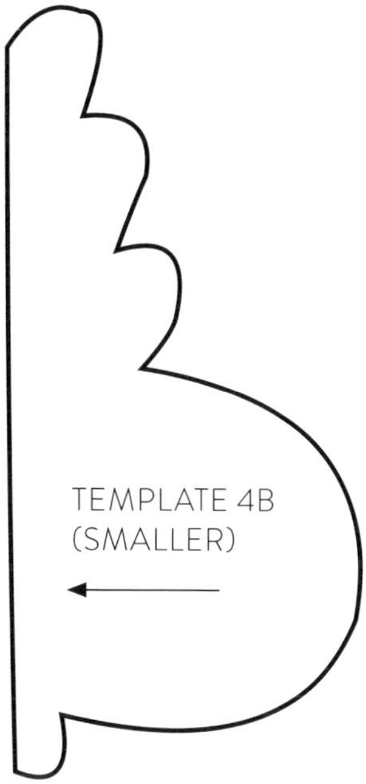

CHRISTMAS ORNAMENTS

**Create beautiful Christmas ornaments that look simple and harmonious —
even though they take some time and are a little finicky to make. The design
can be varied endlessly: large, small, rounded or pointy.**

Level of difficulty: Medium
Time needed: 1 hour

YOU WILL NEED:

Thicker paper
Glue stick
Stronger glue
Crochet hook or knitting needle
String or ribbon for hanging

INSTRUCTIONS:

1. Cut out long strips of paper 1 cm (½ in) wide. The length of the strips will
   determine the size of the ornaments. For a normal-sized ornament (about
   12 cm/4½ in diameter), cut strips that are 15 cm (6 in) long.
2. The number of strips you'll need depends on how you choose to design your
   ornament, but start with 20.
3. Glue each strip into a circle.
4. Choose how you wish to shape the strips. You can flatten the circles to make
   them pointy, fold them in half, keep the circles as they are or make swirls using
   a crochet hook/knitting needle.
5. To make swirls, pick a strip that has not been glued into a circle. Roll the strip
   tightly around the crochet hook or knitting needle and glue the last piece of
   the strip to fasten the roll. If you want the roll to be looser, let it out a little
   before gluing.

6. Now it's time to start creating your ornaments! Glue them together piece by piece using a glue stick to create round patterns.

7. Once you have finished your ornament, you can apply a stronger glue in the centre to stabilise it.

8. Thread the ornament onto a piece of string to hang it.

SPIKY BALL

These spiky Christmas balls originated in Poland, where they are made for Christmas as a reminder of the Star of Bethlehem. In recent years, they have become increasingly popular — and you can see why. They are perfect for decorating your Christmas tree!

Level of difficulty: Advanced
Time needed: 2 hours

YOU WILL NEED:

Thicker paper in a colour and/or pattern of your choosing
Glue stick
Pencil
Small buttons
Needle and thick thread or string

INSTRUCTIONS:

1. Draw and cut out 12 circles in a paper and size of your choosing. For a spiky ball with a diameter of 7 cm (2¾ in), you'll need circles that are 8 cm (3¼ in) in diameter.

2. Fold each circle in half 3 times and unfold to create 8 lines radiating out from the centre point.

3. Draw a smaller circle in the centre of each circle. A coin is the perfect template.

4. Cut along each fold down to the smaller circle.

5. Put some glue in the top right corner of one of the tabs now created. Place the tip of a pencil in the top left corner and roll the tab until you have created a tip. Hold for a moment while the glue hardens. Repeat for each tab, on all 12 circles.

6. With something sharp, make a hole in the centre of each star.

7. Thread one of the buttons onto a piece of strong string, about 40 cm (16 in) long, so that the button is in the middle of the string.

8. Thread both ends of the string through a needle, and thread the needle through the first star with the inside of the star facing up and the outside facing down.

9. Keep going with the remaining 11 stars, threading them so they overlap and the outside faces up.

10. Finally, thread a second button on top of all the stars.

11. Pull on the 2 ends of the string to create a ball and secure it with a couple of knots.

12. Tie a knot for hanging — voilà: the ball is ready!

NEW YEAR'S EVE

*Shooting stars and secret gift boxes
adorn the dining table.*

SHOOTING STARS

A sky full of shooting stars made of paper makes for a dramatic addition to the New Year's table setting. Hang it from a chandelier over the table or as a wall decoration.

Level of difficulty: Medium
Time needed: 1 hour per star
Choose if you want to make individual ornaments or a whole sky full of stars. Follow the instructions to make a single star. If you want to make a sky full of stars, you'll need about 30–40 of them.

YOU WILL NEED:
White paper
Glue stick
Needle and thick thread or string

INSTRUCTIONS:
1. Cut out 8 squares of white paper. The diameter of the finished star will be the same as the dimensions of the squares. Here, we have used squares measuring 8 x 8 cm (3¼ x 3¼ in).
2. Make a 5 mm (¼ in) fold on 2 opposite sides of each paper square.
3. Then fold the squares in half, aligning the folded edges. Unfold.
4. Glue the folded edges and refold so that they stick to each other. Make sure that only the folded edges are glued together.
5. Fold each piece of paper in half to align the short sides.

6. Cut into your desired shape. The template you choose will determine the shape of your star. Feel free to experiment with your own variations, too!

7. Glue in the fold as well as a line running vertically down the middle of the paper, forming a cross. Fold the paper in half and hold until the glue sticks. Be careful not to glue the whole sheet together.

8. Now you have 8 identical folded pieces that, together, will form the star.

9. Glue the pieces together on top of each other by gluing a line vertically down the middle of each piece and horizontally along the bottom (like an upside-down T).

10. Carefully pull the star into shape and glue the last 2 sides together.

11. To string several stars together, thread a needle and string or thread through 2 tips on opposite sides of each star.

STANDING 3D STAR

A striking star that looks great standing on a table but is also beautiful to hang. This star is ideal to make from patterned paper, which is also more forgiving if it doesn't turn out perfectly. Before you begin, set aside both some time and a good deal of patience.

Level of difficulty: Advanced
Time needed: 3 hours

YOU WILL NEED:
Heavyweight card paper
Ruler
Thicker paper in a colour and/
or pattern of your choosing
Glue stick
Stronger glue

INSTRUCTIONS:
1. Trace one of the templates onto card paper. The small template creates a star that is 11 cm (4¼ in) high and the large template one that is 15 cm (6 in).
2. Cut out the piece.
3. Create creases by folding inward along all the lines on the piece. Use a ruler if you need to.
4. Create a flat-sided ball by gluing all the little folded tabs on the piece. Use the palm of your hand to cup the ball until all the glued parts meet and stick.
5. The ball that all the pointy parts will be mounted on is ready. Now onto the tips of the star.
6. Choose a thicker, patterned paper and cut out 20 squares measuring 6 x 6 cm (2½ x 2½ in) for the smaller star and 8 x 8 cm (3¼ x 3¼ in) for the bigger star.

7. Fold the squares along the diagonal into a triangle. Unfold.

8. Fold the sides to meet in the diagonal fold. Unfold.

9. Cut the side opposite to the tip where all the folds meet to give the paper a round shape.

10. Cut about 5 mm (¼ in) into each fold from the round side.

11. Fold down the 5 mm (¼ in) tabs created. Unfold.

12. Glue the inside of one of the outer triangles (see picture on the next page).

13. Fold the piece into a pointy, angular cone by overlapping the glued inside with the outside of the opposite triangle.

14. Fold in the tabs at the base of the cone and use a stronger glue to attach it to the ball. Make sure that the base of the triangular cone fits perfectly onto one of the sides of the ball, which is also triangular. Let the glue harden.

15. Repeat for all 20 cones until the ball is completely covered — and the star is ready.

TEMPLATE: STANDING 3D STAR

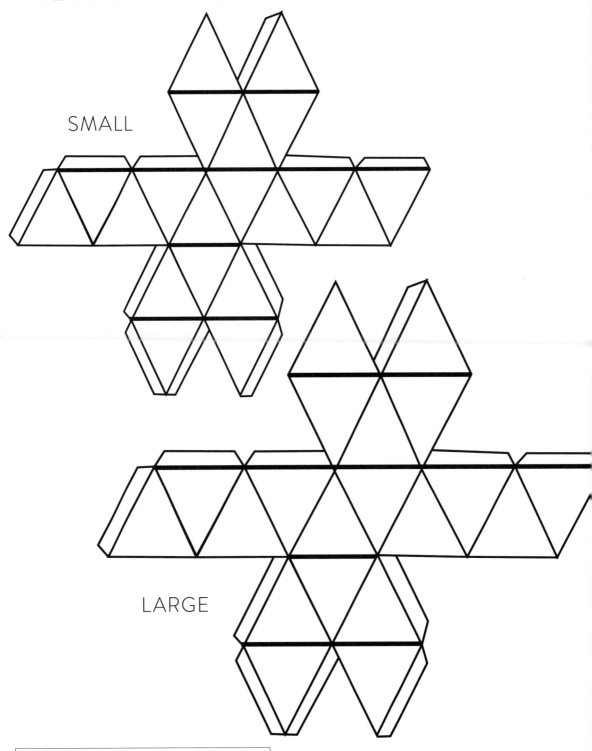

SMALL

LARGE

PAPER GIFT BOX

Surprise your guests with a small gift they can open when sitting down for dinner or coffee. Why not sit some chocolate pralines in a bed of confetti? This paper gift box is guaranteed to be appreciated at your table.

Level of difficulty: Easy
Time needed: 15 minutes

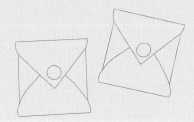

YOU WILL NEED:
Thicker paper in a colour and/or pattern of your choosing

INSTRUCTIONS:
1. Cut a square of paper. The finished gift box will be about half the size. Here, we have used a square that is 22 x 22 cm (8½ x 8½ in), which means that the gift box will be 11 x 11 cm (4¼ x 4¼ in).
2. Fold the paper into a triangle by aligning 2 opposite corners.
3. Fold the triangle in half.
4. Cut one of the tips on the longest side into a half star.
5. At the other tip on the longest side, cut a hole in the folded edge.
6. Fold the triangle once more, aligning the tips with the half star and the hole, thus creating a new, smaller triangle (see picture on the next page).
7. Cut the tip opposite to the long side of the triangle to make it round.
8. Unfold the paper.
9. Place the chosen gift in the middle of the paper.
10. Assemble the gift box by first bringing together the star-shaped tips.
11. Tuck the star-shaped tips through the holes and adjust the gift box to make it straight.

NAPKIN RINGS

Napkin rings with a star theme are a festive addition to your dinner table. If you wish to decorate with identical stars standing upright on the table, cut out 25 stars and glue the first to the last after step 3.

Level of difficulty: Easy
Time needed: 1 hour

YOU WILL NEED:
Thicker paper
Glue stick
Stronger glue

INSTRUCTIONS:

1. Cut out 15 stars in the desired size. You'll need to make them doubled as instructed on the template.
2. Fold the stars in half.
3. Glue along the folded edge of each star and place the stars on top of each other, aligning the folded edges.
4. Cut out a strip of the same paper as the stars measuring 1.5 x 30 cm (⅝ x 12 in).
5. Glue the strip into a circle, wrapping it several times around itself. To give it the right shape and the appropriate size, you can wrap the paper strip around an empty toilet roll.
6. Use a stronger glue to attach the star you made in step 3 to the paper napkin ring.

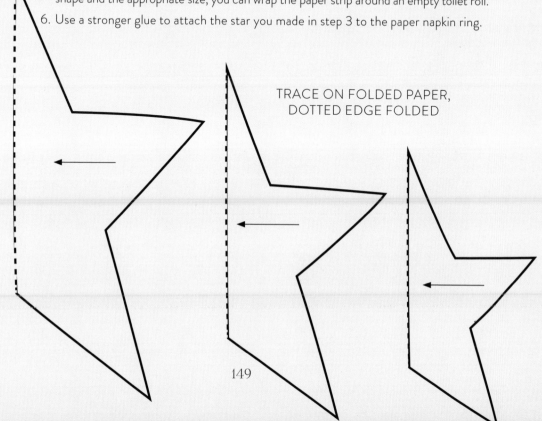

TRACE ON FOLDED PAPER,
DOTTED EDGE FOLDED

HORIZONTAL TABLE STARS

Create a striking table setting with beautiful table stars. All you need is decorative paper. The stars will become quicker to make once you get the hang of them.

Level of difficulty: Medium
Time needed: 15 minutes

YOU WILL NEED:
Thicker paper in a colour and/or pattern of your choosing

INSTRUCTIONS:
1. Cut out a square in your chosen size from the paper. Here, we have used one that is 10 x 10 cm (4 x 4 in).
2. Fold the square in half, with the folded edge towards you.
3. Fold the top right corner down towards the edge nearest you. Unfold.
4. Fold the bottom right corner up towards the edge furthest away from you. Unfold.
5. The folds should now form a cross on the right side of the paper.
6. Fold the lower left corner towards the centre of the cross.
7. Fold the tip that is now in the middle of the cross towards the short side on the left (see picture on the next page).
8. Fold the bottom right corner up towards the edge furthest away from you like the fold you did in step 4.
9. Fold the triangle-like shape you have created in half, so that the side currently facing up becomes the outside with all its folds.
10. Cut from the tip of the short side diagonally towards the folded tip (see picture on the next page) and discard the larger piece. The angle of this cut will determine how narrow the tips of the star will be.
11. Unfold the tip that remains and shape it into a beautiful table star.

152

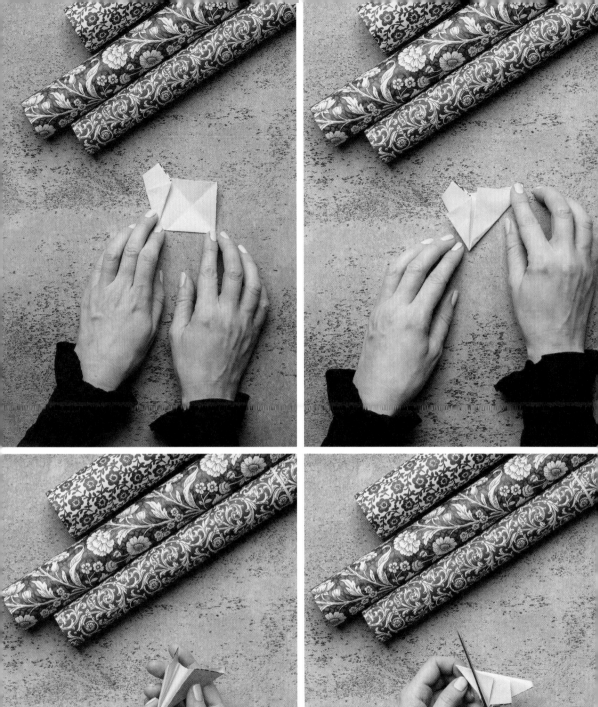

WHEN THE LIGHT RETURNS

Let it bloom inside!

SPRING FLOWER

Make a version of all the advent stars suitable for spring from these templates. Use white baking paper for crisp, neutral flowers or patterned wrapping paper if you want some more colour.

Level of difficulty: Medium

Time needed: 10 hours for a flower using all the templates

Flower from template 1 (22 cm/8½ in diameter): 6 cut-outs

Flower from template 2 (29 cm/11½ in diameter): 6 cut-outs

Flower from template 3 (36 cm/14¼ in diameter): 6 cut-outs

Flower from template 4 (44 cm/17½ in diameter): 6 cut-outs

Flower from template 5 (52 cm/20½ in diameter): 6 cut-outs

Flower from template 6 (58 cm/23 in diameter): 6 cut-outs

The glued folds will be on the back of the flower and cut-outs.

YOU WILL NEED:

Wrapping paper in a colour and/or pattern of your choosing or baking paper

Thicker paper

Glue stick

Stronger glue

INSTRUCTIONS:

1. Trace the templates onto wrapping or baking paper. You'll need to make them doubled as instructed on the template. Make 6 of each.
2. Cut out the pieces just inside the lines.
3. Starting from the longest side, fold the paper pieces horizontally like an accordion, with each fold about 1–1.5 cm (½–⅝ in) wide.
4. Fold each accordion in half. Now complete steps 5–7 for each piece, one at a time.
5. Thoroughly coat the entire inside of the folded accordion with a glue stick.
6. Now pinch the folded accordion together, so that the glued surface is folded in on itself. Hold for a moment, until the sides stick together.
7. Unfold and make sure that only the glued sides are sticking.

8. Now assemble each spring flower individually by first gluing the accordions together in pairs. Hold for a moment, until the sides stick together. Then unfold and make sure that only the glued sides are sticking.

9. Glue the accordions together to form a whole spring flower.

10. Cut out 2 circles for each spring flower in a thicker paper to help stabilise the flower and make it easier to assemble the layers.

11. Glue a paper circle to the centre on both the front and back of each flower with a stronger glue. The smallest flower will sit as the top layer and should only have a paper circle on the back.

12. Now assemble the layers of the spring flower using a stronger glue that you apply to the paper circle on each flower. Then place the spring flowers on top of each other and let the glue harden.

13. If you would like a light source in your spring flower, make 2 identical flowers and follow the instructions under 'Lighting for Stars' on page 83.

TEMPLATE: SPRING FLOWER

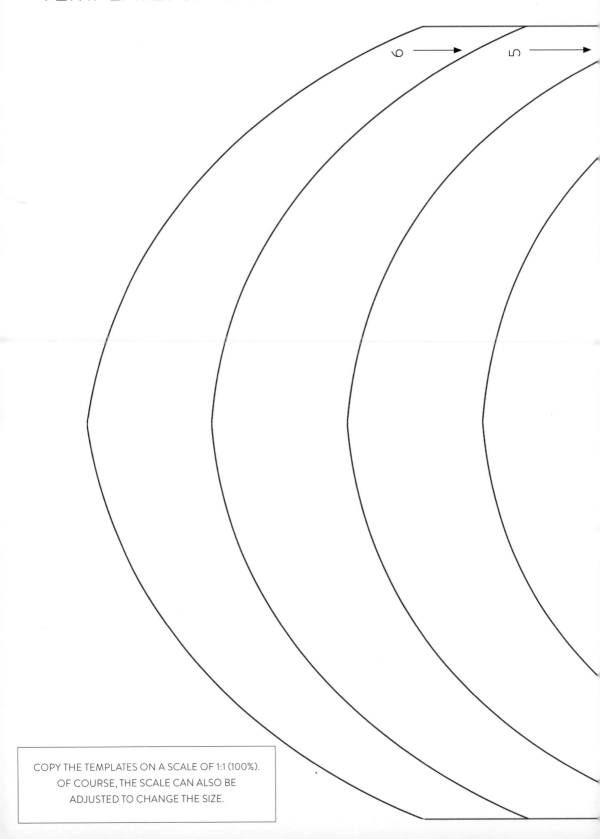

6 →

5 →

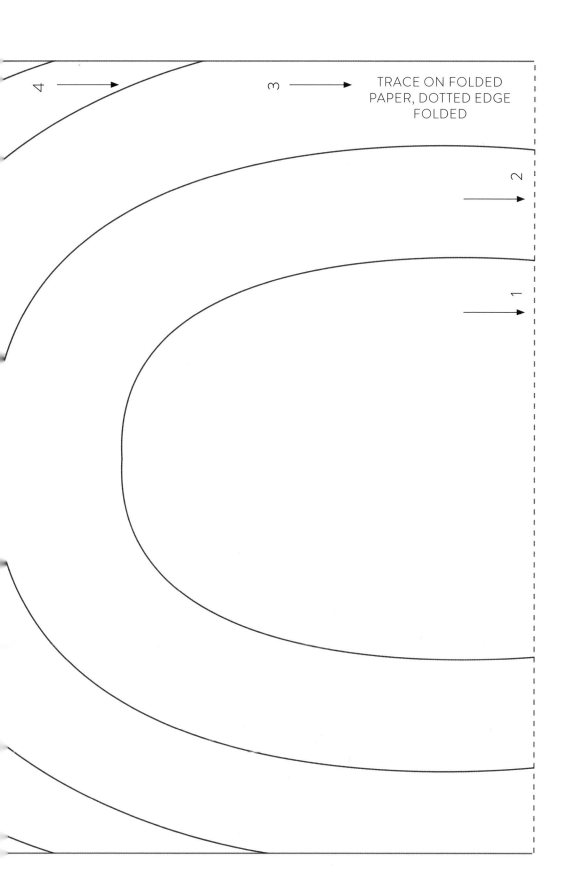

4

3 → TRACE ON FOLDED
PAPER, DOTTED EDGE
FOLDED

2 →

1 →

ANEMONE

Create beautiful anemones out of crêpe paper. These are wonderful as a decoration on a table or windowsill or mounted on a wall. They look even better grouped together.

Level of difficulty: Medium
Time needed: 1 hour per flower

YOU WILL NEED:

Crêpe paper in a colour of your choosing
Small compressed paper balls
Glue stick
Stronger glue

INSTRUCTIONS:

1. Start by tracing the template for the size of the anemone you want to make. You'll need to make them doubled as instructed on the template. Once finished, the larger one will be about 14 cm (5½ in) in diameter and the smaller one about 10 cm (4 in).
2. Trace the template onto crêpe paper, making sure to align the template with the texture of the paper.
3. Cut out the pieces just inside the lines. You'll need 7 pieces for each flower.
4. Gently pull on the paper to make it wider.
5. Fold the pieces lengthways like an accordion, with each fold about 1 cm (½ in) wide.

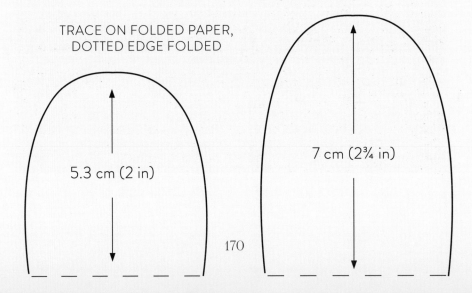

TRACE ON FOLDED PAPER,
DOTTED EDGE FOLDED

5.3 cm (2 in)

7 cm (2¾ in)

170

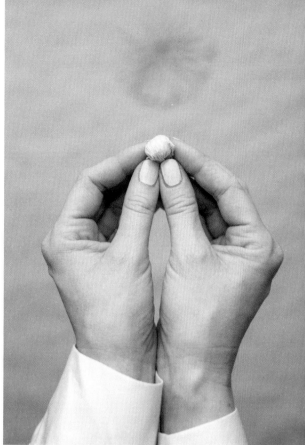

6. Fold each accordion in half. Now complete steps 7–9 for each piece, one at a time.

7. Thoroughly coat the entire inside of the folded accordion with a glue stick.

8. Now pinch the folded accordion together, so that the glued surface is folded in on itself. Hold for a moment, until the sides stick together.

9. Unfold and make sure that only the glued sides are sticking.

10. Now assemble each anemone individually by first gluing the accordions together in pairs. Hold for a moment, until the sides stick together. Then unfold and make sure that only the glued sides are sticking.

11. Glue 7 accordions together to form a whole anemone.

12. Cut out a circle of crêpe paper with a diameter of about 5 cm (2 in). Attach it with a stronger glue in the middle on the back of the flower in order to stabilise it.

13. Take a paper ball and wrap a piece of stretched-out crêpe paper around it. Twist the crêpe paper around the back of the ball and cut it, so that only a stump of paper remains.

14. Attach the covered paper ball using a stronger glue in the centre of the flower, with the stump facing down into it.
15. Once the glue has hardened, shape the flower by cupping it and gently pulling on the petals.

DAHLIA

Dahlia season usually runs from midsummer until autumn, but you can extend it by crafting flowers out of paper. Try making your dahlias in different types of paper, both plain and patterned.

Level of difficulty: Medium
Time needed: at least 5 hours
Small dahlia (29 cm/11½ in diameter):
Round circle, 15 cm (6 in) diameter
7 cm (2¾ in) squares for petals, 80 pieces
Medium-sized dahlia (35 cm/14 in diameter):
Round circle, 20 cm (8 in) diameter
9 cm (3½ in) squares for petals, 90 pieces
Large dahlia (45 cm/17¾ in diameter):
Round circle, 25 cm (10 in) diameter
11 cm (4¼ in) squares for petals, 100 pieces

YOU WILL NEED:

Paper in a colour and quality of your choosing – here, we have used crêpe paper
Thicker paper
Glue stick

INSTRUCTIONS:

1. Choose the size of dahlia you want to make.
2. Cut out squares from your paper, adjusting the size and number to your chosen dahlia. If you are using crêpe paper, cut the squares in half, turning them into rectangles instead. Make sure that the texture of the paper runs lengthways along the rectangle. Then pull on the rectangles to expand them into squares.
3. Fold one corner almost towards the centre of the square.
4. Fold the opposite corner almost towards the centre, making it overlap with the first to create a rounded cone.
5. Glue the inside of the overlap, refold and hold until the glue sticks, flattening at the pointier end to make it easier to glue and then to stick to the circle base.

6. Repeat steps 3–5 for each square.

7. Cut out a circle in the thicker paper. The diameter of the circle will depend on the size of dahlia you have chosen to make, see the list on page 177.

8. One at a time, glue the cones to the circle with the tips towards the centre. Start with the outermost layer.

9. When the outermost layer is in place, attach the next layer of cones, overlapping with the first. Continue layer by layer, until you have filled the entire circle and created your dahlia.

BRANCH IN BLOOM

Create beautiful branches in bloom that will keep for a long time and stay pristine with no need to water! The pretty flowers are made from coffee filters pinned to a branch. If you wish, you can paint them with watercolours or diluted food colouring.

Level of difficulty: Easy
Time needed: 15 minutes per flower

YOU WILL NEED:
White coffee filters
Sewing pins
Branch without flowers

INSTRUCTIONS:
1. Trace each of the 3 templates onto coffee filters.
2. Cut out the pieces just inside the lines. There will automatically be 2 of each, as coffee filters come in 2 layers.
3. Place all 6 circles on top of each other, with the largest at the bottom and the smallest on top.
4. Push a sewing pin through the centre of all 6 circles, beginning with the smallest.
5. Shape and crease each circle separately to create the petals on the flower.
6. Insert the sewing pin with the flower lengthways into the branch and voilà — you have created a branch in bloom! Add as many flowers as you want.

TEMPLATE: BRANCH IN BLOOM
& WREATH OF CARNATIONS

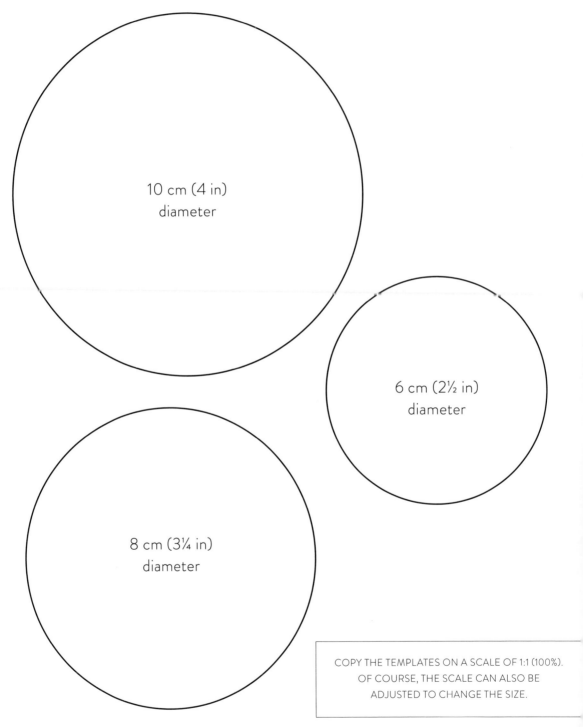

10 cm (4 in)
diameter

6 cm (2½ in)
diameter

8 cm (3¼ in)
diameter

COPY THE TEMPLATES ON A SCALE OF 1:1 (100%).
OF COURSE, THE SCALE CAN ALSO BE
ADJUSTED TO CHANGE THE SIZE.

WREATH OF CARNATIONS

Isn't it amazing what beautiful and elegant crafts you can make simply from materials found in your local supermarket? This wreath of blooming carnations is easily made from folded coffee filters. If you wish, you can paint them with watercolours or diluted food colouring.

Level of difficulty: Easy
Time needed: 10 hours for a large wreath

YOU WILL NEED:
White coffee filters
Sewing pins
A wreath base made of straw

INSTRUCTIONS:

1. To cover a straw wreath that is 55 cm (22 in) in diameter, you'll need flowers from about 150 coffee filters. If you choose a wreath with a smaller diameter, you'll need fewer coffee filters and it'll be quicker to make.
2. Trace each of the 3 templates on page 182 onto coffee filters.
3. Cut out the pieces just inside the lines. There will automatically be 2 of each, as coffee filters come in 2 layers.
4. Place all 6 circles on top of each other with the largest at the bottom and the smallest on top.
5. Push a sewing pin through the centre of all 6 circles, beginning with the smallest.
6. Shape and crease each circle separately to create the petals on the carnation.
7. Sink the whole sewing pin with the carnation into the straw base.
8. Repeat steps 2–7 until you have covered the entire wreath with your coffee filter carnations.

STORAGE

IT'S NOW TIME TO CAREFULLY PUT AWAY all the beautiful crafts you have made. Some crafts you may want to keep around all year, while others can be carefully stored away in boxes, ready to be taken out when darkness begins to fall once more. Both hat boxes and old trunks are perfect for storage. If you don't have access to good boxes, you can always store larger items and big stars high up on cupboards or other furniture.

Don't throw away anything you have made – always save your papercrafts. If you didn't have time to finish a project, you can always pick up where you left off next year. Perhaps you'll get new ideas during the year to come and want to build on something you have already made. Did any of the stars come apart? If you combine them, perhaps you can create something new.

When you pick up your creations again in a few months, you may need to supplement them with a little glue – and adjust their tips and shapes. Other than that, your crafts will be just as beautiful as when you put them away.

Remember: when it comes to your creativity, the sky is the limit.

With love, Jennie and Cecilia

THANK YOU

First, we want to extend a big and loving thanks to our steadfast husbands, Mårten and Sebastian, for taking care of both logistics and children, and showing great patience with your busy wives. You are a big reason that we were able to finish this book project. We love you so very much.

Another big thank you to the Museum of Västernorrland in Härnösand, Sweden, for allowing us access to the beautiful interiors in the Court House and the Old School at Murberget, where we shot the majority of the photographs. Thank you to Fiestad Farm BnB, FatJosie Keramik and Emelie Vänervik for opening your doors and letting us use your premises. An additional thank you to Marion and ERNST Form for lending us props.

Thank you sweet mum Carina, dad Håkan and Engla for cutting out pieces, making additional crafts and preparing props for our photo shoots. Without you, there simply would not have been enough time.